Early

Prevention

Dr. Yi Song

ISBN: 979-8-9948506-3-3 (print)

Regeneration Effect Publishing

This is Book Two of

Regeneration Effect :

Sacred Wisdom for Staying Young

EARLY PREVENTION
BOOK 2

....

The ***Yellow Emperor's Classic of Medicine***—one of the oldest and most important texts in Chinese medicine—describes the importance of prevention and treating diseases before they arise.

"Treating disease only when it arises is like trying to dig wells when the fire already spreads

or forging weapons when the

war already starts.”

Sadly, in the past twenty years of

practicing, **I've found that most**

people have no interest in

making an effort toward
early prevention.

Most people today believe
that modern Western
medicine has a solution for
every problem—no matter
when it appears.

Got high blood pressure?

There's a pill for that.

Cholesterol too high?

Another prescription.

In this mindset, there's little incentive to take responsibility early. Many see no real issue with eating processed foods, drinking regularly, smoking, or avoiding exercise. Deep down, they know these habits are harmful, **but comfort has become their normal.** The thought of giving up what feels good now for the sake of a healthier body years later feels too distant, too abstract.

And change—real change—takes effort.

Real transformation begins with a decision: **You have to *want* to change.**

Because change only happens when the pain of staying with

the status quo finally outweighs the pain of making changes.

You don't have to wait for a crisis. Early prevention is powerful.

The sooner you start, the better.

But even if you've already experienced a decline in health, it's not too late to make a shift. Your body is still listening. It still wants to heal. It just needs the right tools, the right rhythm, and your commitment to show up consistently.

This book isn't about perfection.

It's about *presence*.

About showing up for your body with care and curiosity. About giving yourself the chance not just to live longer—but to *live better*. To reach your 70s, 80s, even 90s with clarity, strength, mobility, and joy.

Not just a lifespan, but a health span.

That's what we're building here—one story, one habit, one transformation at a time.

I once told someone, "I want to be skinny by summer." He looked at me and said, "How long did it take you to get fat?"

It wasn't the answer I wanted. But it was the answer I needed.

Change takes time.

You can't reverse years of imbalance overnight.

Some things you can stop cold turkey—sugar, alcohol, maybe even a bad habit—but **deep healing takes time.**

Especially when it involves the prenatal blueprint you were given.

Transformation asks something of us—new habits, different foods, better boundaries, or rest where we once pushed through.

It may mean slowing down, letting go of coping mechanisms, or rebuilding routines that feel foreign at first. In the beginning, change can feel like friction.

The nervous system may resist, not because it's wrong, but because it's new.

For individuals with genetic predispositions—such as heart disease, cancer, or metabolic disorders —this awareness becomes even more important.

Patterns can be inherited, but they don't have to be repeated.

Lifestyle shifts can influence how genes express themselves.

Small, consistent choices—

nourishment, movement, breath work,

sleep, mindset—can help redirect the

body toward repair rather than decline.

Selena Gomez is a powerful example of how much stress and environment can influence a genetic predisposition. She developed lupus at a young age—**not because she did anything "wrong,"** but because she grew up under enormous pressure. From early childhood, she was performing, touring, recording, attending appearances, and constantly facing public scrutiny.

The body can only carry that level of stress for so long before something shifts.

Autoimmune conditions like lupus don't appear overnight.

They build slowly, often beginning with subtle signs: fatigue, digestive imbalance, inflammation, emotional exhaustion, or recurring infections. When someone has a genetic tendency toward autoimmunity, chronic stress can act like a switch—

awakening dormant patterns and accelerating dysfunction. The body, overwhelmed and unable to regulate, begins to misidentify its own tissues as a threat.

Selena's journey eventually led to a kidney transplant, a life-saving intervention.

But if the underlying drivers— stress, exhaustion, systemic inflammation—aren't addressed, the body remains in

survival mode rather than healing mode.

Selena has openly shared her experience with anxiety and depression, both of which are common companions to autoimmune disease because the nervous system and immune system are deeply intertwined.

It's important to recognize that she was incredibly young when all of this began.

Most teenagers and young adults

don't have the language or awareness

to understand what their body is

telling them—especially when they're

in a high-performance environment

where slowing down feels impossible.

At that age, symptoms are

often brushed off, pushed

through, or normalized.

If her predisposition had been

identified earlier—if someone had

helped her understand the emotional,

neurological, and physical stress load

she was carrying—she might have been able to support her immune system before it reached the point of organ damage.

Early intervention doesn't always prevent a diagnosis, but it can change the progression dramatically.

Her experience reminds us of a universal truth:

The body keeps score.

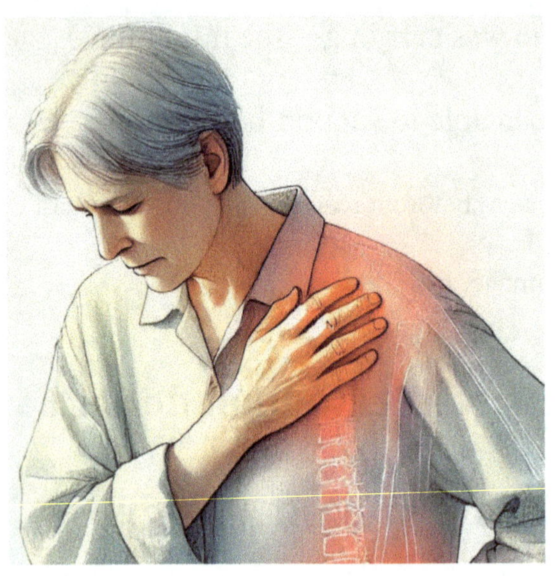

It responds to pressure, imbalance, self-neglect, and unprocessed stress just as it responds to nourishment, rest, and repair. Genetics may open the door, but lifestyle, emotional environment, and stress determine how far the condition progresses.

These inherited patterns don't define your future, but they do influence how stress, environment, diet, and lifestyle show up in the body over time.

This isn't to diminish science. It's to remind us that science and

nature were never
meant to be at odds.

When they walk
together,

that's when true

healing becomes
possible.

Ancient Chinese philosophy teaches that everything follows a natural cycle.

Ebbs and flows, expansion and contraction, tailwinds and headwinds.

It reminds us that ***nothing stays static,***

and that trying to force life into a straight line—constant productivity, constant youth, constant energy—only leads to exhaustion, frustration, and resistance.

But when you learn to **move *with* the rhythms of nature,** rather than against them, life becomes something else entirely: more easeful, more intuitive, more sustainable. And that shift doesn't just affect your mindset.

It shapes your **health**, your **career**, your **relationships**, and your **sense of purpose**.

Think of it like rowing a boat: push too hard against the current, and you tire quickly. But if you time your strokes with the tide, you go farther, faster. With far less effort.

Instead of fighting against aging, stress, and the inevitable changes that come with life, **what if you embraced a different approach?**

Recognizing your body's rhythms one of the most profound acts of self-respect.

Some days your energy will peak.

Other days your body will ask you to

rest, to slow down.

Your body doesn't respond the

same way in winter as it does in

summer.

Hormones, digestion, mood,

and metabolism all shift with

the seasons.

And with the stages of life.

Learning to work *with* those

changes is key to long-term

vitality.

To get in-depth discussion about Early Prevention, please follow the link or scan the QR code to preorder "Regeneration Effect: Sacred Wisdom for Staying Young" and learn how you can implement all the principles in your life.

https://bundle.regenerationeffect.com

ABOUT THE AUTHOR

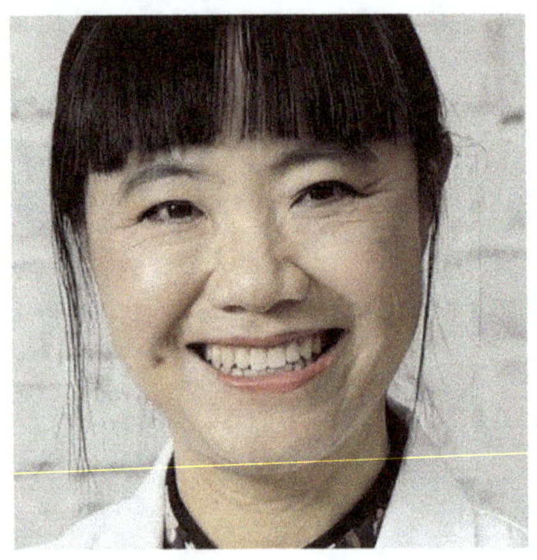

Dr. Yi Song was born and raised in Beijing, China, into a family with seventeen generations of experience in both Chinese and Western medicine. Twenty-eight years ago, she came to the United States to study pathology at Brown University. After observing the shortcomings of symptom-focused treatments, Dr.

Song returned to her roots to focus on true regenerative healing — addressing disease at its source. She has had a holistic clinic in Boston since 2004. In 2018, she founded the Zenerchi Retreat in Medellin, Colombia. Her introduction to stem cell therapy in 2020 was marked by her mother's successful treatment and subsequent independence at age 81. Dr. Song believes that stem cell therapy aligns with holistic principles and is the author of "Regeneration Effect: Sacred Wisdom for Staying Young" and the series of seven books in "The Six Principles to Natural Longevity". Her vision is to combine stem cell therapy, Traditional Chinese

Medicine, and anti-aging treatments to help people live a long, high-quality life. She offers advanced stem cell treatments at Zenerchi Retreat in Colombia not available in the US. You can also get consultation about your conditions and concerns in person in Boston or at our network of doctors in the US and online.

www.ingramcontent.com/pod-product-compliance
Lightning Source LLC
Chambersburg PA
CBHW050817160726
48004CB00002B/893